DISCARD

D1377929

MEASURING TIME: THE CALENDAR

By Julia Vogel • Illustrated by Luanne Marten

The Child's World

Published by The Child's World®
1980 Lookout Drive • Mankato, MN 56003-1705
800-599-READ • www.childsworld.com

Acknowledgments
The Child's World®: Mary Berendes, Publishing Director
The Design Lab: Cover and interior design
Amnet: Cover and interior production
Red Line Editorial: Editorial direction

Photo credits
Shutterstock Images, cover, 1, 15, 20; Feng Yu/Shutterstock Images,
cover, 1, 2; iStockphoto, 5; David Scheuber/Shutterstock Images, 9;
Galyna Andrushko/Shutterstock Images, 11

ISBN 9781614732815
LCCN 2012933669

Printed in the United States of America
Mankato, MN
July 2012
PA02121

ABOUT THE AUTHOR
Award-winning author Julia Vogel spent weeks, months, and years studying biology in college and forestry in graduate school. Julia has four kids and a dog that barks at the moon.

ABOUT THE ILLUSTRATOR
Luanne Marten has been drawing for a long time. She earned a bachelor's degree in art and design from the University of Kansas. She has a dog named Millie who arrived on the first day of the year 2000.

TABLE OF CONTENTS

Counting Down the Days

What days do you look forward to? Summer vacation? Halloween?

Clocks help you count seconds, minutes, and hours. But they don't help for counting how long until your birthday.

You need a calendar for that. Calendars measure days, weeks, months, and years.

Calendars help you remember events and special days.

Long ago, daytime marked the workday.

Sun and Moon

We haven't always had calendars. Long ago, people used the sun and the moon to keep track of passing days. Some people woke up with the sunrise. They went to sleep with the sunset. That was one day. People made marks on bones or pieces of bark to keep track of the passing days.

Moon Gazing

Other people counted days by watching the moon. You can, too. Go outside every night and draw the moon. Each night, you will see it has changed shape just a bit. But at the end of 29 and a half days, it will look just like it did at the beginning. This is one **moon cycle**.

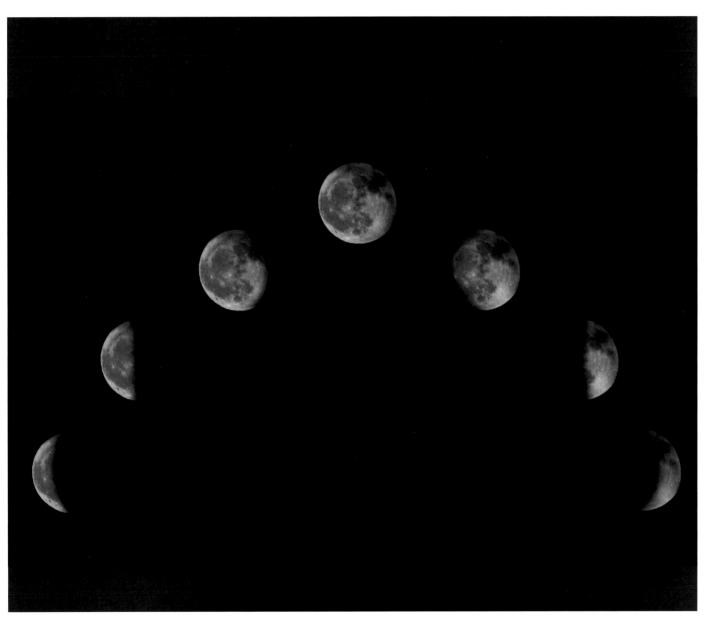

During one month, you can see these different shapes of the moon.

The First Calendars

In fact, the first calendars were **lunar** calendars. One moon cycle equaled one month. But the lunar year did not have enough days in them. Soon the calendar got off track from the seasons. The calendar may have said it was summer. But it was really winter!

A lunar calendar that got off track could have said this was summer.

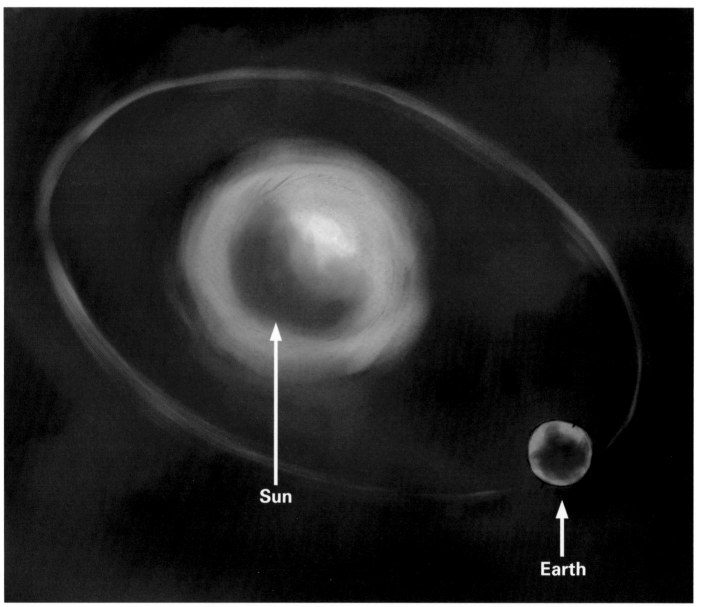

Sun

Earth

The time it takes Earth to travel around the sun is one **solar** year.

Solar Power

A calendar that was more correct was the solar calendar. It measured a year by how long it took Earth to travel around the sun. The calendar was about 365 days. This is what today's main calendar is, too.

Weeks

Soon people split up the days in each month. The Babylonians grouped days into sevens. They called each group a week. The **ancient** Romans liked this system. They named one day of the week after the sun: Sunday. They named another after the moon: Monday.

But people got confused sometimes. There was no set number of weeks or days in a month.

NAME THE DAYS! The days of the week are: Sunday, Monday, Tuesday, Wednesday, Thursday, Friday, Saturday. If today is Tuesday, and your friend wants to meet you three days from now, which day will you meet? Count forward three days: Wednesday, Thursday, Friday. Your friend wants to meet you on Friday!

The sun and the moon are important for calendars.

Julius Caesar made changes to the calendar.

Romans to the Rescue

The Roman leader Julius Caesar wanted to fix this. He had a calendar made. It had 365 and one-fourth days split into 12 months. Each month had a set number of days.

Some of the names of our months come from this time. January is named after Janus. He was the Roman god of beginnings. July is named after Julius Caesar.

Calendars of the World

The Gregorian calendar is the calendar used in most of the world. The Gregorian calendar adjusted the calendar Julius Caesar had made just a bit. Chinese and Hebrew calendars are also common. They are lunar and solar calendars combined.

YEARS
Each year has a number in the Gregorian calendar. The United States became a country in 1776. What year were you born?

In the Chinese calendar, each year is tied to one of 12 animals.

JANUARY

Su	Mo	Tu	We	Th	Fr	St
1	2	3	4	5	6	7
8	9	10	11	12	13	14
15	16	17	18	19	20	21
22	23	24	25	26	27	28
29	30	31				

FEBRUARY

Su	Mo	Tu	We	Th	Fr	St
			1	2	3	4
5	6	7	8	9	10	11
12	13	14	15	16	17	18
19	20	21	22	23	24	25
26	27	28	29			

MARCH

Su	Mo	Tu	We	Th	Fr	St
				1	2	3
4	5	6	7	8	9	10
11	12	13	14	15	16	17
18	19	20	21	22	23	24
25	26	27	28	29	30	31

APRIL

Su	Mo	Tu	We	Th	Fr	St
1	2	3	4	5	6	7
8	9	10	11	12	13	14
15	16	17	18	19	20	21
22	23	24	25	26	27	28
29	30					

MAY

Su	Mo	Tu	We	Th	Fr	St
		1	2	3	4	5
6	7	8	9	10	11	12
13	14	15	16	17	18	19
20	21	22	23	24	25	26
27	28	29	30	31		

JUNE

Su	Mo	Tu	We	Th	Fr	St
					1	2
3	4	5	6	7	8	9
10	11	12	13	14	15	16
17	18	19	20	21	22	23
24	25	26	27	28	29	30

JULY

Su	Mo	Tu	We	Th	Fr	St
1	2	3	4	5	6	7
8	9	10	11	12	13	14
15	16	17	18	19	20	21
22	23	24	25	26	27	28
29	30	31				

AUGUST

Su	Mo	Tu	We	Th	Fr	St
			1	2	3	4
5	6	7	8	9	10	11
12	13	14	15	16	17	18
19	20	21	22	23	24	25
26	27	28	29	30	31	

SEPTEMBER

Su	Mo	Tu	We	Th	Fr	St
						1
2	3	4	5	6	7	8
9	10	11	12	13	14	15
16	17	18	19	20	21	22
23/30	24	25	26	27	28	29

OCTOBER

Su	Mo	Tu	We	Th	Fr	St
	1	2	3	4	5	6
7	8	9	10	11	12	13
14	15	16	17	18	19	20
21	22	23	24	25	26	27
28	29	30	31			

NOVEMBER

Su	Mo	Tu	We	Th	Fr	St
				1	2	3
4	5	6	7	8	9	10
11	12	13	14	15	16	17
18	19	20	21	22	23	24
25	26	27	28	29	30	

DECEMBER

Su	Mo	Tu	We	Th	Fr	St
						1
2	3	4	5	6	7	8
9	10	11	12	13	14	15
16	17	18	19	20	21	22
23/30	24/31	25	26	27	28	29

The 12 months in the Gregorian calendar

NAMES OF THE MONTHS

Can you name the months in order? January, February, March, April, May, June, July, August, September, October, November, December. Try to memorize them. Then each month you'll know where you are in the year.

Months, Days, and Years, Oh My!

January 1, 2015. That's one way to write a date. Or you can use only numbers to write the same date: 1/1/2015. That is month/day/year. How do you write today's date? Try it both ways.

Track the Dates

Does your classroom have a wall calendar so you know what day it is? You might have a calendar in your home, too. That way no one in your family misses an appointment or a birthday!

Calendars on computers and cell phones are also useful. You can add your school assignments and friends' birthdays to it. Then make it send you reminders. You won't miss anything when you use calendars to help you.

Practice memorizing these important calendar numbers.

Glossary

ancient (AYN-shuhnt): If something is ancient, it is very old. Ancient Egyptians started their days at sunrise.

lunar (LOO-nur): If something is lunar, it has to do with the moon. Long ago, people used lunar calendars.

moon cycle (MOON SYE-kuhl): A moon cycle is the time it takes for the moon to pass through all its phases, or 29 and a half days. Some calendars are based on a moon cycle.

solar (SOH-lur): If something is solar, it has to do with the sun. Some calendars are solar calendars.

Books

Kummer, Patricia K. *The Calendar*. New York: Franklin Watts, 2005.

Maestro, Betsy. *The Story of Clocks and Calendars*. New York: HarperCollins, 2004.

Williams, Brian. *Measuring Time*. North Mankato, MN: Smart Apple Media, 2003.

Web Sites

Visit our Web site for links about measuring time with calendars: **childsworld.com/links**

Note to Parents, Teachers, and Librarians: We routinely verify our Web links to make sure they are safe and active sites. So encourage your readers to check them out!

Index